COMPETITIVE SPORTS SERIES

SWIMMING

Eddie Gorton

Batsford Academic and Educational Ltd   London

Typeset by Tek-Art Ltd, London SE20
and printed in Great Britain by
R.J. Acford
Chichester, Sussex
for the publishers
Batsford Academic and Educational Ltd
an imprint of B T Batsford Ltd
4 Fitzhardinge Street
London W1H 0AH

British Library Cataloguing in Publication Data

Gorton, Eddie
    Swimming.—(Competitive sports series)
    1. Swimming
    I. Title II. Series
    797.2'1   GV837

ISBN 0 7134 4079 1

Contents

Foreword

Despite the fact that there are numerous books on swimming now on the market, regrettably few of these offer in-depth advice or guidance to those who have gained some degree of proficiency in swimming and wish to acquire and develop the techniques which will help them to achieve success in competitive swimming.

Eddie Gorton is to be congratulated, therefore, on producing this comprehensive and well-illustrated book to fill a much-felt need. In it not only are all strokes, starts and turns admirably dealt with, but in addition there are sections on swimming fundamentals, the principles of training and coaching drills.

As a National Development Officer for the Amateur Swimming Association for many years Eddie Gorton has been able to draw on a wealth of experience of teaching and coaching at all levels up to international standard. He has also in the course of his work visited many parts of the world and observed the coaching methods used by eminent coaches and the training methods of Olympic swimming stars.

Consequently he is able to write with authority and offer practical advice which should be welcomed by swimming teachers, coaches and all who are interested in improving standards of performance.

I have no doubt that they will find this ASA approved publication a most valuable teaching and coaching aid and I warmly commend it to them.

J M Noble
Chairman, ASA Education Committee

Introduction

This book is directed towards those swimmers, teachers and coaches requiring up to date knowledge of speed swimming. It is intended as an introduction to training methods, modern mechanics of swimming and modern aspects the competitive strokes with their starts and turns.

Ultimate success is the culmination of dedicated work which links natural and acquired skill with the physiological and psychological training of the swimmer.

Although there is not a special chapter devoted to psychological training, it is hoped that it will not be completely ignored.

It must be realised that each swimmer should have some goal at which to aim. Without this, training lacks purpose and will rarely be successful. It becomes more realistic if the aim can be divided into short, medium and long term. It is not realistic to have an immediate aim to win the club championship if the swimmer has just swum 50 metres for the first time.

Many swimmers take part in races without adequate mental preparation. It is useful if the race is rehearsed in the mind beforehand, especially before the day of the race. It should be done many times so that the swimmer will not only be prepared but will have much greater confidence.

A typical race rehearsal may be thought out as follows: *before the start* (loosen up, keep warm, breathe naturally); *at the start* (be alert, concentrate); *entry into water* (stretch); *first half of race* (do not rush the stroke, build up power); *the turn* (do not slow down, stretch away from the wall); *second half of race* (maintain stroke, be strong); *the finish* (be determined, it should hurt).

Many people consider swimming as an individual sport, but every effort should be made to develop team spirit. This is most important and should be encouraged from the vocal support given to team mates to the wearing of team costumes and sweatshirts showing team identity.

Without team spirit, fun and enthusiasm will be lacking and so will success. Nothing helps more than the support and encouragement of the rest of the team.

Fundamental Aspects of Swimming

Two important aims of good swimming are the development of propulsion and the reduction of resistance.

PROPULSION

This aspect of swimming can be subdivided into the improvement of personal strength and the improvement of a swimmer's 'feel' for the water.

There are many ways of improving strength. The obvious ones are best suited to training in a gymnasium with special equipment. Swimming itself strengthens the body especially when practised often. Gradually extending the distance and intensity of the sessions will certainly result in an increase of strength.

In addition to the acquisition of strength, special mention must be made regarding flexibility. Attention should be given to maintaining and increasing the range of movements of all joints. Good flexibility certainly aids propulsion in swimming.

Before explaining how a swimmer improves 'feel' for the water, it is important to understand what 'feel' means. It is the ability a swimmer has to feel pressure on the hand, created by the flow of water as the hand and arm are pulled through the water.

Some swimmers develop it quite quickly and naturally; others have to swim regularly and often to acquire it.

Before attempting to explain how 'feel' for the water actually comes about, it is useful to observe really good swimmers in action from underwater. It is noticeable that in every case the arm movements follow curved pathways (figure 1).

Not only is it important to observe good swimmers in action, it is also useful to look at and understand ways by which boats are propelled. Other than by sail (using the power of the wind), there are two main examples, which are the paddle-type action, and the propeller action.

(a) FRONT CRAWL   (b) BACK STROKE

(c) BREAST STROKE   (d) BUTTERFLY

Figure 1   Typical arm movements used when swimming the competitive strokes.

PADDLE

As the flat blade of the paddle is pulled through the water, there is a build-up of pressure of water in front of the paddle, which eventually finds its way around to the back of the paddle forming a wake of low pressure (figure 2).

8

Figure 2   Paddle action

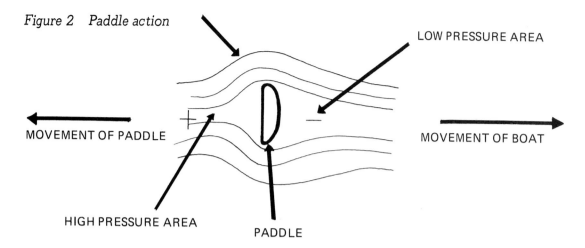

LOW PRESSURE AREA

MOVEMENT OF PADDLE

MOVEMENT OF BOAT

HIGH PRESSURE AREA

PADDLE

As a result, the boat moves in the opposite direction to the movement of the paddle. (Whenever there are two different areas of pressure in close proximity to each other there is always movement from the higher pressure area to the lower one.)

If a hand is substituted for the paddle, it illustrates how the swimmer gets propulsion using movements similar to those of the paddle (figure 3).

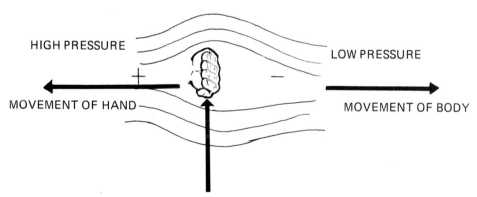

HIGH PRESSURE

LOW PRESSURE

MOVEMENT OF HAND

MOVEMENT OF BODY

HAND FROM UNDERNEATH OR FROM THE SIDE (FRONT CRAWL)

Figure 3   Hand movement through water (similar to paddle)

PROPELLER

Before studying the action of a propeller it is important to understand how the wing of an aeroplane helps to lift it off the ground. The shape and angle of the wing causes the air which is flowing over its top surface to follow a curved pathway and the air which is flowing underneath to follow a straight and unobstructed pathway. This action creates high pressure under the wing and low pressure above it which creates lift (figure 4).

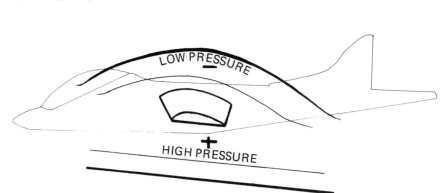

DIRECTION OF MOVEMENT (LIFT)

LOW PRESSURE

HIGH PRESSURE

Figure 4   *Air movement over aeroplane wing which creates differing pressures above and below wing.*

The propeller of an aeroplane, helicopter or boat is constructed in such a way that the pitch of the blade passing through the air or water creates high pressure on one side of the blade and low pressure on the other, in very much the same way as an aeroplane wing gives lift.

In closely observing the blade of a propeller it is seen that it is specially shaped and angled. The pitch is angled approximately $30°$ to the direction of the movement of the blade, which causes the flow of water or air passing over the blade to alter creating differing pressures on one side of the blade to the other. Because movement always takes place from high pressure to low pressure a propeller moving in a horizontal plane will provide a vertical lift like a helicopter (figure 5). A propeller moving in a vertical plane will provide horizontal lift which is either forwards or backwards (figure 6). Because movement is always achieved at right angles to the movement of the propeller, a combined forward and upwards movement would be possible if the propeller were to spin at an angle other than horizontal or vertical.

A similar technique to the propeller is used by the sculling action of a swimmer. Provided the angle, pitch and speed of the hand and forearm is correct, movement can be obtained in any direction (figures 7 and 8).

Figure 5   *Air movement over propellers which creates differing pressures above and below the propellers*

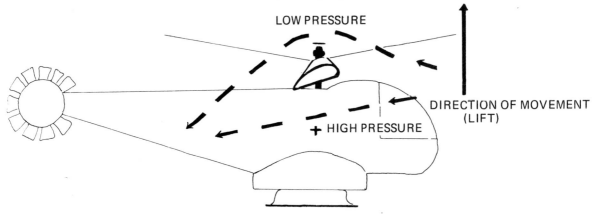

LOW PRESSURE

HIGH PRESSURE

DIRECTION OF MOVEMENT (LIFT)

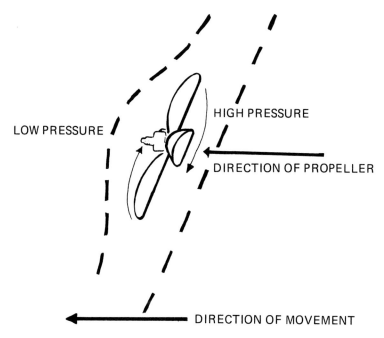

LOW PRESSURE

HIGH PRESSURE

DIRECTION OF PROPELLER

DIRECTION OF MOVEMENT

Figure 6   Propeller spinning in vertical plane

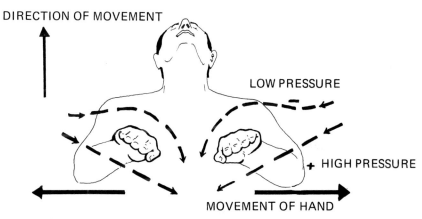

DIRECTION OF MOVEMENT

LOW PRESSURE

+ HIGH PRESSURE

MOVEMENT OF HAND

Figure 7   Sculling hand and arm moving outwards

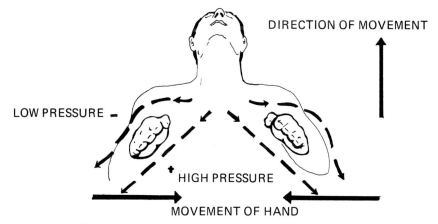

DIRECTION OF MOVEMENT

LOW PRESSURE

HIGH PRESSURE

MOVEMENT OF HAND

Figure 8   Sculling hand and arm moving inwards

At the beginning of this chapter it is stressed that the best swimmers pull in curved pathways. Closer observation of the angle pitch and speeds of the hands and forearms shows that propulsion is obtained by a combination of a paddle action and an adapted propeller action.

The early swimmer therefore, should be encouraged to experiment with a wide variety of sculling actions so that he can naturally combine the two propulsive actions of paddle and propeller to the best effect. It is not sufficient to allow novice swimmers to swim short distances and stop them because the stroke does not look perfect. FEEL for the water will only come about when swimmers are given plenty of opportunity to experiment and swim longer distances. The distance to be swum should depend on a swimmer's endurance and efficiency of breathing, rather than whether the stroke looks correct.

RESISTANCE

The main natural advantage a swimmer possesses that helps to reduce resistance is buoyancy. It is the physical make-up of bone, fat, muscle and connective tissue, balanced by the upthrust present in water, which determines the swimming position.

A simple test to determine whether a person is a good floater is to lie flat on the water either on front or back. A good floater will remain flat and high on the water. A poor floater will sink low or the angle of the body will alter and the legs will drop.

There is not a great deal a person can do to counteract this except to make sure that special attention is given to technique, especially to the position of the head and the leg kick if the legs tend to sink.

Every swimmer should try to adopt a flat horizontal swimming position. However, it would be a mistake to force the head down too deeply in attempting to attain it. Not only would breathing become more difficult but the hips and legs would tend to rise too high to compensate for the low head (figures 9, 10 and 11).

Resistance will be aggravated if there is any lateral movement of the lower body. The aim should be to swim in a straight line. Care should be taken when breathing and when recovering the arms in frontcrawl. The arms often cause the hips and legs to swing sideways if the movements are carelessly executed (figure 12).

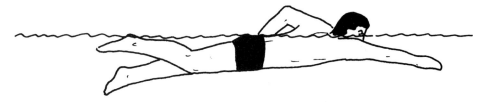

Figure 9   A good efficient position in the water

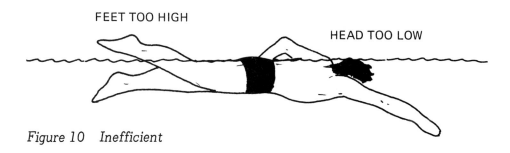

FEET TOO HIGH

HEAD TOO LOW

Figure 10   Inefficient

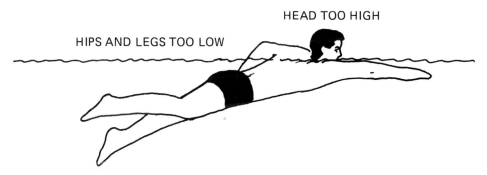

HEAD TOO HIGH

HIPS AND LEGS TOO LOW

Figure 11   Inefficient

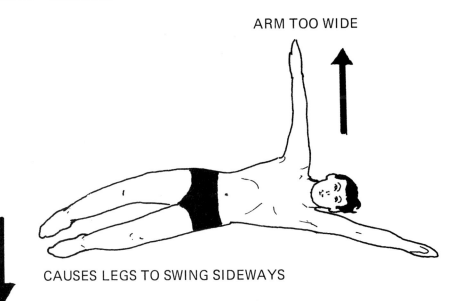

ARM TOO WIDE

CAUSES LEGS TO SWING SIDEWAYS

13

Figure 12   Inefficient — causes legs to swing sideways

Front Crawl

Front crawl is the fastest of all swimming strokes. The alternating action of the arms, which use the strong muscles of the upper back and chest, maintain constant propulsion throughout the pulling movements.

The leg action contributes to the overall speed of the stroke, but does not provide it as effectively as the arm action.

Although there are many variations of swimming front crawl, there are two main differences, which are to be described and these are called the six beat stroke and the two beat stroke. All other styles come somewhere between these two extremes.

THE SIX BEAT STROKE

This stroke is characterised by a swimmer who kicks six times while the arms complete one full cycle. The speed of the arms is relatively slow and there is an appearance of power in the action. The leg kick also has an

Six beat front crawl

appearance of power and rhythm and contributes greatly to the overall speed of the swimmer.

Most speed swimmers tend to use this style of swimming, but there are noticeable exceptions.

BODY POSITION

The head and shoulders are high in relation to the water. The bow wave, the size of which is caused by the speed of the swimmer, meets the face at the hair line and should then separate and pass on either side of the head in a trough just below the ears.

The shoulders give the impression of being slightly above the water, and this is emphasised as each shoulder is aternately raised during recovery and lowered during propulsion.

The hips are high in water in order to eliminate resistance, but they should not be so high that they break through the water. The feet reach from the surface to a point approximately 18 in. (45 cm) below. The depth will depend on the size and flexibility of the swimmer, and the effectiveness of the kick (figure 13). (Note: six beats can be managed if the feet separate considerably less than 18 in. (45 cm) but the arm action has to be quickened to accommodate for this and therefore they and the legs tend to become less effective).

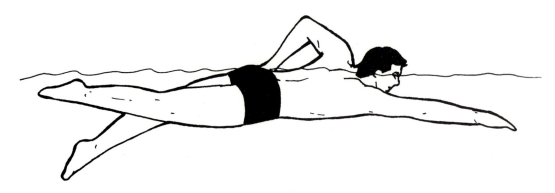

Figure 13   A good body position

ARM ACTION

ENTRY

The entry into the water is made with the fingers, hand and forearm entering in that order. It helps if the hand is slightly turned so that the thumb enters the water first. The point of entry is towards the centre line of the body in front of the face. The arm should be comfortably stretched, but not straight at the moment of entry (figure 14).

Figure 14   Hand entry   *Figure 15   Catch or purchase*

CATCH

After the hand and arm sink into the water, the arm is straightened to a point along the centre line approximately 6 in.-9 in (15 cm-21 cm) below the surface, with the palm of the hand facing the floor of the pool. Pressure should then be exerted on the water with a firm wrist in a downwards and backwards direction. In order to accomplish this, the wrist is flexed and the arm begins to bend so that the elbow remains relatively high in the water (figure 15).

PULL

The pull now begins and progresses smoothly and powerfully from the 'catch'. The arm continues to bend until a 90° angle is reached under the shoulders. At this point, the hand is usually somewhere underneath the opposite shoulder (figure 16). Variations of this movement are seen among swimmers, but all of them should have the main characteristics of a well bent arm with a high elbow and a pull movement towards the opposite shoulder. It is noticeable with very good swimmers during the latter stages of this movement that there is a slight acceleration of the hand and forearm and an angle of pitch of the hand which takes advantage of 'lift'.

Figure 16   Pull action   *Figure 17   Pushing action*

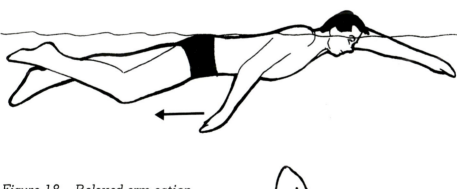

Figure 18   Relaxed arm action

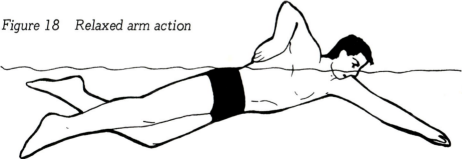

PUSH

From this point, the arm is extended towards the feet, the hand and forearm maintaining pressure on the water (figure 17). The hand moves across the body during this movement. As the arm nears full extension the hand is turned so that the little finger comes uppermost and the arm is lifted out of the water with the elbow leading, which starts the recovery method.

RECOVERY

This movement should be completed with as little tension as possible. In the six beat stroke the elbow is carried *high* above the water and the forearm is always maintained below the level of the elbow. The aim is to carry the hand from hip to entry in a straight line. Obviously this is very difficult and success will depend on the degree of flexibility the swimmer has in the shoulder region (figure 18 and photograph 1).

Photograph 1   Arm recovery (note the high elbow and relaxed action)

The relationship between the movement of one arm with the other is very important in the six beat stroke. It is characterised by a noticeable catch up of one arm on the other during the push and recovery movement.

At the point of entry of one hand, the other is approximately under the shoulders. As the arm which has just entered, stretches forward, the other extends backwards and at one phase in the stroke both are stretched. The backward arm is now recovered and enters the water as the other is under the shoulder (figure 19).

Figure 19   Timing of one arm with the other (six beat)

LEG ACTION

The leg action has three main functions which are to provide propulsion to balance the reaction of the arms and breathing actions and to maintain the body in a horizontal and streamlined position.

An efficient leg kick is obtained when the feet and ankles can be hyper-extended, and the movement is continuous and powerful. It is essential when swimming this style of front crawl for the leg kick to have these character-istics.

Generally speaking, most propulsion is obtained from the downward action but the upward action is important. The downward action is performed with a moderately bent leg. However, during the final action towards the lowest point, the leg is powerfully and speedily straightened. The upward action is performed with a straight leg until the leg nears the surface when the leg is moderately bent in readiness for the downward kick (figure 20).

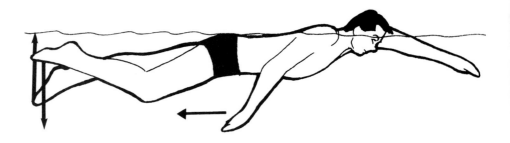

Figure 20   Leg action

BREATHING

Attention to breathing, whether it is the manner of taking a breath or the movement of the head prior to, during and after taking a breath, should never be neglected.

Most swimmers breathe naturally but if any problems are apparent, these are usually caused by inadequate exhalation and great care should be devoted to correcting this.

The movement of the head is important, it should be done quickly and in a manner that does not cause the remainder of the body to twist sideways. The head should be turned sideways when one arm is at full extension but exerting pressure on the water, the other arm should be just beginning the recovery at the point of taking the arm out of the water (breathing can happen slightly later during the recovery of the arm but this can create a jerky movement which is to be avoided). (Figure 21)

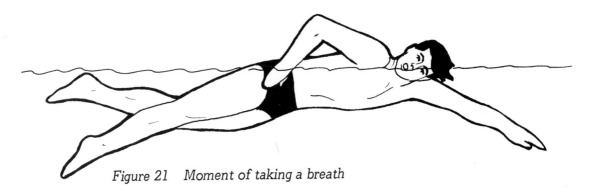

Figure 21   Moment of taking a breath

TIMING

Each leg will kick three times for each arm movement. Most swimmers adapt naturally to the timing in a stroke. Normally the downbeat occurs when the arm on the same side of the body is just completing the propulsive phase.

THE TWO BEAT STROKE

This stroke is characterised by a swimmer who kicks the legs twice to one complete arm cycle.

It is mostly swum by naturally buoyant swimmers who have no difficulty in maintaining a horizontal and streamline position. Girls often fall into this category, therefore it is not uncommon to see them swimming in this way. Children, for the same reasons find this style of swimming suits them. (It must be stressed, however, that as childrens' bodies develop, what may have been acceptable at a young age may not suit them during adolescence.)

The position of the head and shoulders is a little lower in the water, although emphasis should not be placed on trying to achieve this by adopting a forced position.

ARM ACTION

The speed of the arm action is usually quicker than that of the six beat, and the impression is one of continuous propulsion. As in the 'six beat', the entry is made — fingers, wrist, elbow — in that order. The propulsion action is made with a high elbow, and there is the same deviation from the centre line.

The forward extension after the entry is not so pronounced and the 'catch' is made sooner. The recovery is made earlier in that the arm is not extended as far back towards the hips.

Finally, the catch up is not as noticeable, as one arm enters the water the other has progressed well beyond the shoulder (figure 22).

Figure 22 Timing one arm with the other (two beat)

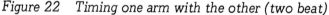
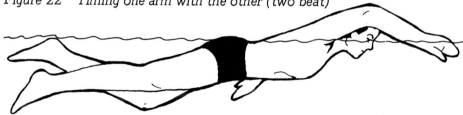

The recovery action above the water does not have the same emphasis on high elbows. Although the elbows are still the highest part of the arms, the movement to entry is more rounded.

The remaining actions in the stroke do not differ, even the action of the leg kick is the same with the exception of speed and number of kicks to the arm action.

Breast Stroke

Breaststroke in its recreative form is a relaxing, easy way of swimming but in its racing form is highly technical and physically demanding.

BODY POSITION

The position of the body changes throughout the arm, leg and breathing actions.

Usually the head is high with the eyes looking forward through the water at a point approximately 2 in. (5 cm) below the surface. From the head, the body is angled so that the hips are lower than in other strokes, which means the legs can be bent on recovery without breaking through the surface.

In recent times there has been emphasis on changing the body position throughout the stroke, which has resulted in it being swum with a body action, similar to the dolphin action of the butterfly stroke.

When this style of swimming is adopted, the head and shoulders are raised higher out of the water at the moment of breathing, than is normally the case. This action tends to make the hips sink, which is overcome to a certain extent by those swimmers who are very flexible in the spine. In order to correct this and help the hips to rise the arms are stretched forward and pressed downwards, when they are recovered, at the same time the head is pressed slightly downwards into the water.

It is important to understand that a swimmer who lacks flexibility in the

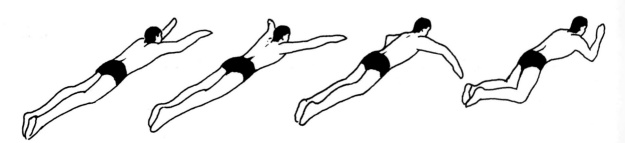

The breast stroke cycle

spine might have difficulty in adopting this style of breaststroke.

The normal driving action of the legs, which takes place at this time, also has the effect of raising the hips.

ARM ACTION

Part 1   This section refers to the type of arm action normally used when swimming the undulating type of breast stroke and part 2 refers to the arm action normally used when swimming the more traditional type of stroke which is best used by a swimmer who has powerful arms and shoulders who achieves good propulsion from the arm action, and one who lacks flexibility in the spine.

The arm action commences with the arms fully extended in front of the shoulders at a depth of approximately 6 in.-8 in. (15 cm-20 cm). The thumbs are usually touching with the little fingers slightly raised. (Figure 23)

The arms are pulled sideways with the hands tilted in such a way that the little fingers are raised higher than the thumbs and the wrists are slightly fixed. (The tilting of the hands is known as the pitch and the angle is approximately 30°, see Chapter 1 and figure 8 (sculling).

Figure 23

If the pitch of the hand and the flexion of the wrist is correct, water will flow over the back and palm of the hand from the point of the little finger to the joining of the thumb to the wrist. This action will tend to keep the upper body high in the water by providing horizontal lift.

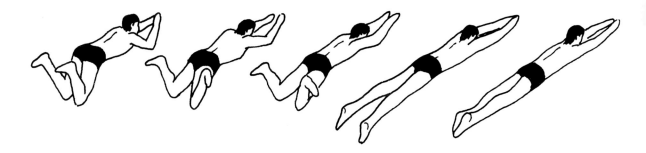

The sideways movement continues until the hand passes outside the elbows. (It is important to concentrate on increasing the speed of the hand movement during this action, especially towards the end of the outward movement.)

The outward movement changes with a powerful swirling action to an inward one with the elbows maintaining a high position in the water. The forearm is now below the elbow and it is the thumb edge of the hand which is in front of the little finger. The water now flows over the back and palm of the hands from the thumbs and the first fingers to the joining of the little finger with the wrist. (It is now important to concentrate on accelerating the inwards movements of the hands) (figure 24.) It is this action which now provides horizontal lift in a forward direction.

Figure 24   Inward movement of arms in propulsive phase

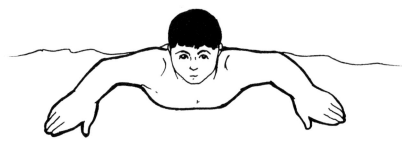

Photograph 2   End of inward movement of arms and elbows and a breath is taken

The inward movement continues until the thumbs are almost touching, when the hands are pushed forward to extension. (Care should be taken to maintain the inwards movement of the elbows after the hands begin to push forward. It is this movement which is so important in cutting down resistance of the elbows. See photograph 2.

Part 2   The arm pull commences in the same way as in part 1 and remains a similar action until the forearms pass outside the elbows. At this point the hands and forearms are pulled under the elbows and are pressed backwards towards the feet using a paddle action (figure 3.) This backward movement is a powerful one and continues until the hands and forearms are in line with the shoulders. (Figures 25 and 26.) They are then brought together in a circular movement before they are moved forward to the stretch position.

Figures 25 and 26   Arm actions of a swimmer strong in arms and shoulders

26

LEG KICK

The importance of the leg kick in breast stroke cannot be over-emphasised. It is the only stroke which uses the kick when the arms are not involved with a propulsive movement. In fact, in many cases, the legs have to work against a retarding movement caused by a badly timed arm movement.

The legs are recovered from a fully stretched position, which is relatively deep in the water. Therefore, the first action is a lifting one, especially of the lower legs. During this movement the feet are extended and streamlined and remain so as the knees bend and the feet are brought up near the seat to a point when the feet are directly above the knees.

25

At this stage, the feet are turned sideways so that the instep and lower leg are able to press on the water as the legs are driven backwards and sideways. (The more the feet can be turned sideways during this early stage of the kick the better.)

The angle of attack of the sideways and backwards kick is approximately 45° and is maintained until the legs are almost straight. At this point, the movement is changed to an accelerating inwards one until the legs are fully extended.

This latter part of the kick is known as the whip action (figures 27 to 33.)

Figures 27 to 33   Leg action

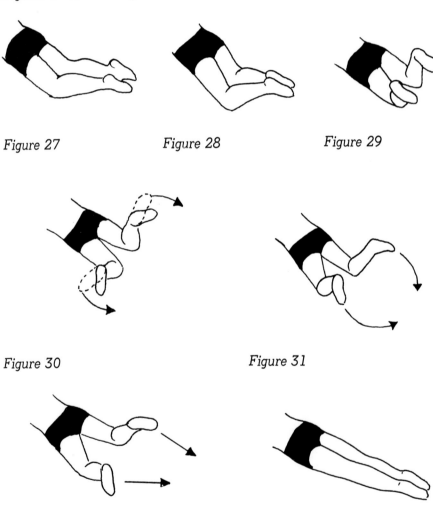

Figure 27   *Figure 28*   *Figure 29*

Figure 30   *Figure 31*

Figure 32   *Figure 33*

BREATHING

The point of inhalation should occur towards the end of the inwards sculling movement of the arms as the mouth naturally comes out of the water. Exhalation takes place after the head is lowered back into the water. (Figure 34).

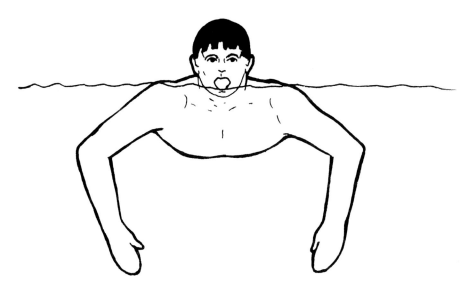

Figure 34   Moment of breathing

TIMING

Timing is probably the most important aspect of the stroke. Without perfect timing it is almost impossible to swim breast stroke really well.

Breast stroke is actually a pulling action of the arms as the legs are stretched and streamlined and a pushing action with the legs as the arms are stretched and streamlined.

From a fully streamlined position of both arms and legs. The arms pull as the legs remain stretched. Both the arms and legs recover at the same time. (This is the time of least propulsion, therefore care must be taken not to do either movement with pressure.) The arms reach full extension and the legs drive the body forward. (Figures 35-40).

Figure 35   Arms stretch forward   Legs stretch backward

Figure 36   Arms pull   Legs stretch backward

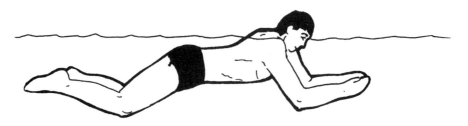

Figure 37   Arms recover (i)   Legs recover (i)

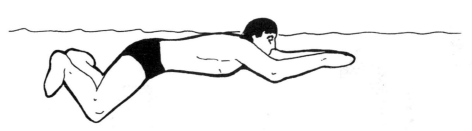

Figure 38   Arms recover (ii)   Legs recover (ii)

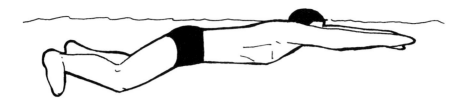

Figure 39   Arms stretch forward   Legs propel

Figure 40   Arms stretch forward   Legs stretch backward

Figures 35 to 40   Timing sequence of breast stroke

Back Stroke

Back crawl is by far the most popular stroke in speed swimming on the back and is now the only stroke used competitively.

It is similar to front crawl in that an alternating action of the arms is used and the legs alternate in an upwards and downwards kick timed with the arm stroke. Compared with front crawl, however, it is a slower stroke because of the mechanical disadvantage of the pulling muscles of the upper back and chest.

BODY POSITION

The stroke is best performed when the body is held in a slight saucer shaped position from head to feet.

The head should be raised sufficiently to prevent water from passing over the face. In order to achieve this the chin is tucked into the top of the chest

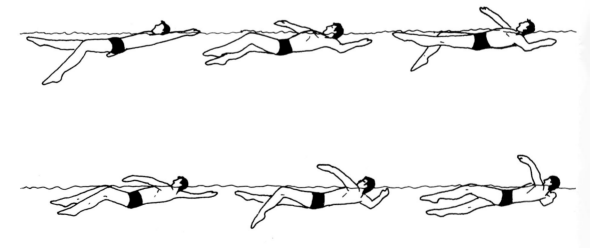

Complete sequence of back strokes

without any undue tension. This tends to raise the back of the head so that the water separates and flows on either side of the head just below the ears.

The hips are high in the water but not so high that the knees break through the surface and disturb the water.

The feet at the highest point come to the surface creating turbulence (figure 41).

Figure 41   Good body position

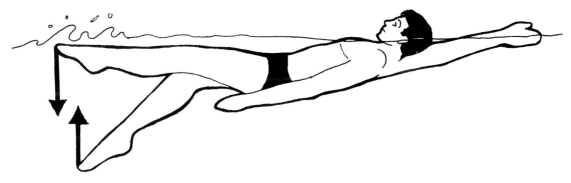

The shoulders roll so that one shoulder is slightly out of the water at the time of the arm recovery, while the opposite shoulder is submerged quite deeply in the water during propulsion (figure 42).

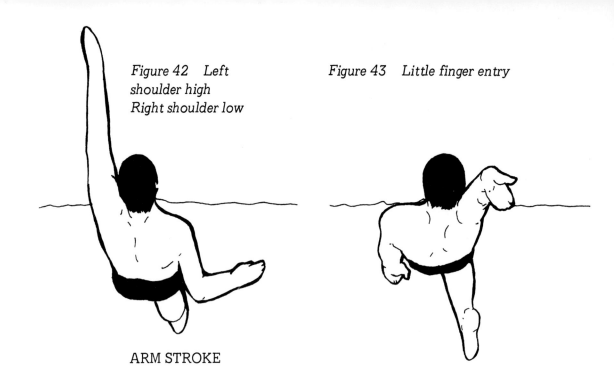

Figure 42   Left shoulder high Right shoulder low

Figure 43   Little finger entry

ARM STROKE

ENTRY

The entry is made with a straight arm behind the centre of the head. It is best if the little finger enters the water before the rest of the hand. Some swimmers however, who are less flexible in the shoulders, enter with the back of the hand first. When this happens, it is important that the hand is turned so that the thumb becomes uppermost, as the hand and arm sink into the water (figure 43.)

CATCH

After the entry the arm remains straight and presses downwards and outwards away from the centre line. The hand should be turned sufficiently so that the palm exerts pressure on the water during this downward and outwards movement. When the hand has travelled approximately 12in. (30cm) the wrist is flexed and the pressure on the water is increased (figure 44.)

PULL

At this point the palm of the hand is turned towards the feet and the elbow begins to bend. The hand is now relatively low in the water.

The elbow continues to bend as the hand moves towards the feet and rises. (During this movement it is important that the hand catches up with the elbow and that the elbow does not lead the arm movement towards the feet) (figure 45.)

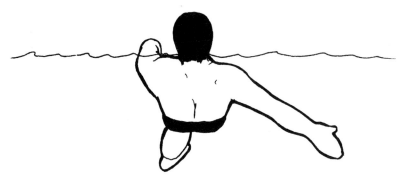

Figure 44   Early propulsive phase

Figure 45   Hand and arm alongside shoulder

Most of the pulling movement is performed with the hand moving in an upwards and backwards manner; the uppermost point of which occurs when
the elbow is bent at about 90° and is alongside or just past the shoulder.

PUSH

The arm is now extended downwards in a strong pushing action, which is
continued until the arm is fully extended at a point just below the hips, the
palm of the hand facing towards the floor of the pool (figure 46).

Figure 46   End of pushing action

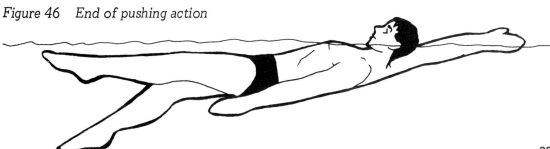

RECOVERY

At the end of this pushing movement the hand and wrist are smoothly turned so that the palm faces inwards and the thumb is uppermost, (some swimmers turn the palm outwards and the little finger uppermost) and is then raised out of the water. The movement continues in a high semi-circle so that the hand follows a straight line from hips to entry behind the head. About half way through this action, the arm is rotated so that the palm of the hand is turned outwards ready for entry (figure 47) (If the little finger is the first to come out of the water, the arm is already rotated and ready for entry.)

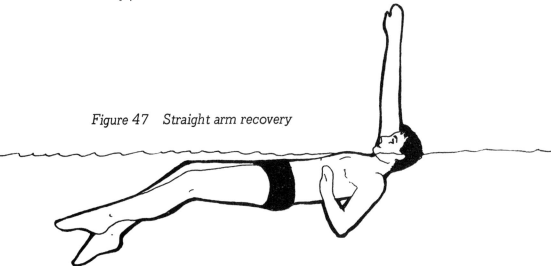

Figure 47   Straight arm recovery

TIMING OF THE ARMS

It is important that the entry of one hand coincides with the final push phase of the other. When this happens the body is fully extended from finger tip to finger tip. Without this the stroke is jerky and does not have the long smooth action which is typical of good swimming (figure 48).

Figure 48   Stretch from entry of right arm to finish of propulsion of left arm

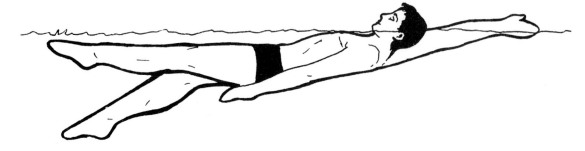

LEG KICK

The back crawl leg kick is an important aspect in the correct performance of this stroke, since not only does it balance the stroke and maintain stream-lining but it also affords considerable propulsion, especially when the swimmer has flexible ankles.

The leg action is similar to front crawl except that most of the propulsion is obtained from the upward movement. For most of this upward kick the knees are bent and for most of the downward action are kept straight (figure 49).

Figure 49   Leg action

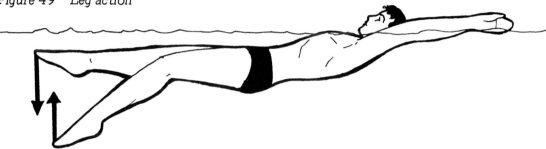

One other noticeable difference is that, there is a tendency for the legs to kick sideways to the left and right as well as up and down, as a reaction to the strong pull of the arms.

BREATHING

Breathing does not normally present problems unless the body position is incorrect and water washes over the face, or that the arm recovery is so performed as to throw a curtain of water over the face.

It is essential, however, that breathing is regular and deep. Most swimmers adapt to their own pattern, which usually means breathing in as one arm passes the head and out as the other passes the head.

TIMING

Unlike front crawl the only effective timing is six beats of the legs to one complete cycle of the arms. Any other should be discouraged.

Butterfly

The butterfly stroke is bettered for speed only by the front crawl. It is a symmetrical stroke which requires suppleness and flexibility of the body and power in the shoulders and arms.

BODY POSITION

The body is flat and horizontal but, because of the nature of the stroke, an undulating body action is created.

The top of the head leads the way except for breathing. The shoulders are relatively high throughout most of the stroke otherwise a swimmer would have difficulty in recovering the arms and create too much resistance. There is a problem as the arms re-enter the water just after the head drops after inhalation has finished. This is the point at which the shoulders are deepest in the water and care must be taken to prevent the swimmer from sinking.

Butterfly stroke sequence

The hips should remain close to the surface throughout but the undulating movement causes their position to change from a position at the surface to a depth of approximately 6 in.-9 in. (15 cm-22 cm).

At the top of the kick, the feet come to the surface (it is noticeable that, with some very good swimmers, the feet break through the surface) and are at a depth of 24 in. (60 cm) at the lowest point (figure 50).

Figure 50   Body position

ARM ACTION

ENTRY
The entry is similar to front crawl in that fingers, wrist and forearm enter in that order. It is best if the hand is turned so that the thumb is slightly depressed to enter the water before the rest of the hand. Normally the entry of both arms is slightly wider than the shoulder (figure 51).

Figure 51   Arm entry

CATCH

After the entry is made the hands sink slightly in the water, the wrists are flexed and begin a sideways movement similar to the outward scull of breast stroke.

PULL

This initial sideways action is then linked to a downwards movement and the elbows bend and continue to bend during this sideways and downward action. The movement continues until the hands are slightly outside the elbows (figure 52). The arms are then pulled inwards and backwards (figure 53) to a point when the elbows are bent at 90° which occurs when the hands have just passed underneath the shoulders (figure 54).

Figure 52   Outward movement of pull

Figure 53   Inward movement of pull

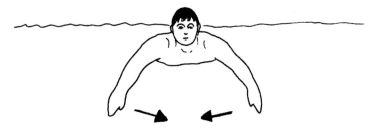

Figure 54   Position of arms under body during propulsion

PUSH

The arms are now extended backwards and sideways with the palms pressing on the water. Before full extension is reached the palms turn inwards. The pull and push action is similar to a keyhole shaped movement (figure 1(d)).

RECOVERY

At the same time as the palms turn inwards to face the hips, the arms are lifted out of the water to start the arm recovery. This final movement is a rigorous one which aids the recovery action.

After the arms are clear of the water they are swung sideways over the water in a rounded action back to entry.

LEG KICK

The leg kick is important for two reasons. In the first place, it gives tremendous propulsion to the stroke and secondly the downwards action of the legs causes the hips to rise, therefore eliminating much of the body resistance which is caused by the hips sinking.

The kick is performed in exactly the same way as frontcrawl except that both legs drive at the same time. Propulsion is gained from the powerful downwards action, which is mainly performed with bent legs while the upwards action is mainly performed with straight legs.

BREATHING

Breathing should take place towards the end of the pushing action of the arms (figure 55). This is the point at which the body is moving the fastest and the upper body is highest in the water. At this point the neck is extended and the mouth comes clear of the water. It will remain so after the arms have started the over-water recovery (figure 56 see photograph 3).

The head returns to the water after the hands have passed the shoulder and will be slightly ahead of the entry of the hands (figure 57).

Figure 55   Moment of breathing

Figure 56   High position at start of arm recovery

Photograph 3   After the powerful propulsive action the body appears to fly

Figure 57   Arm recovery. Head is dropping

TIMING

The legs kick twice to one arm cycle. The downbeat of the kick occurs when the arms enter the water and the second downbeat occurs as the arms are well into the pushing action (figures 58-62).

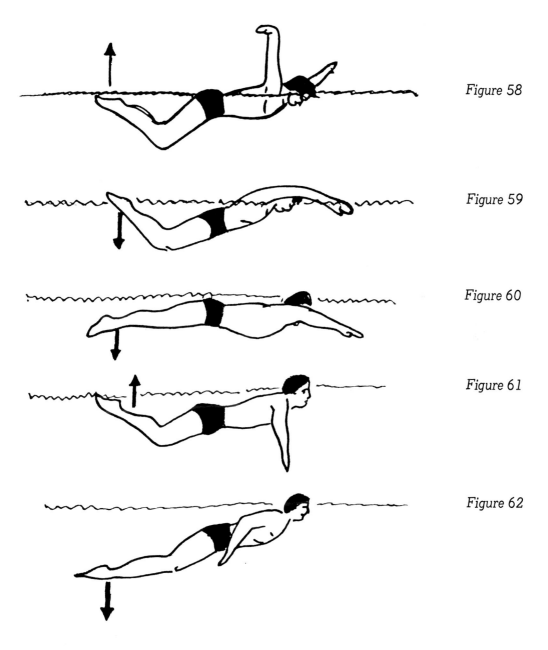

Figure 58

Figure 59

Figure 60

Figure 61

Figure 62

Figure 58 to 62   Timing of leg kick with arm movements

Coaching drills

Coaching drills are practices which encourage stroke accuracy, which means that a swimmer can be helped and encouraged to maintain good techniques from day to day and week to week, through hard training sessions and most important of all during important competition swims.

Drill practices should always start with swimming the whole stroke, following which emphasis is placed on sections of the stroke which are usually performed as progressive practices. Finally, time should be allowed so that these drills can be integrated into the full stroke.

FRONT CRAWL AND BACK CRAWL

KICKING DRILLS
   (i) Kicking practice holding a kicking board at arms length.
  (ii) Kicking practice with arms extended in front.
 (iii) Kicking practice with one arm extended in front, the other by the side, (alternate leading arm).
 (iv) Some of these practices can be done on the side.

PULLING PRACTICES
   (i) Normal swimming but with pull buoy supporting hips.
  (ii) Single arm practice with pull buoy supporting hips (alternate arms). There are many combinations of this, eg pull four right arms then four left — pull alternate lengths right arm then left arm.
 (iii) Pull with a catch up, ie pull with one arm while the other remains stretched then pull with the other arm while the other is stretched out in front.

KICKING AND PULLING DRILLS
Repeat the practices as for pulling but practice the leg kick at the same time.

BUTTERFLY

KICKING DRILLS
   (i) Dolphin kicking while holding a float at arms' length.
   (ii) Dolphin kicking with both arms stretched out in front.
   (iii) Dolphin kicking with both arms by the sides at the hips.
   (iv) Some of these practices can be done on the back and on the side.

PULLING PRACTICES
   (i) Pulling practices with hips supported with a pull buoy.
   (ii) Single arm pulling practices (although butterfly is a simultaneous stroke, provided the arm is recovered with a straight arm, and is carried high above the water, the action helps the recovery in the stroke.
   (iii) Combination movements are useful.
       ie two single pulls left arm followed by two pulls right arm, followed by two complete pulls.

KICKING AND PULLING DRILLS
Repeat the activities for pulling but the leg kick is practised at the same time.

BREAST STROKE

KICKING DRILLS
   (i) Kicking with the arms stretched forward and holding a kicking board.
   (ii) Kicking with the arms stretched forward.
   (iii) Kicking with arms stretched behind or at the hips.

PULLING PRACTICES
   (i) Pulling practice with hips supported with a pull buoy.
   (ii) Single arm pulling with hips supported with a pull buoy, other arm stretched forward.

KICKING AND PULLING DRILLS
   (i) Practice combinations of kicking and pulling, ie kick three times to every pull.
   (ii) Pull, kick, then emphasise stretch and glide.

It is best if swimmers adopt a regular routine for each stroke. In this way the drill becomes a set pattern and is easily and effectively performed.

A typical drill section for the improvement of the arm action within a training schedule might be as follows:

Swim 4 x (6 x 25 metres)   *first 25 metres* pull left arm only with other arm extended in front of body.

second 25 metres pull right arm only with other arm extended in front of body.

third 25 metres alternate 4 strokes left arm only then right arm only with other arm extended in front of the body.

fourth 25 metres alternate one stroke left arm only then one stroke right arm only with other hand extended in front of body (known as catch up swimming).

fifth 25 metres alternate one stroke left arm only then one stroke right arm only but start pull of the opposite arm just before the other arm enters the water.

sixth 25 metres swim normal but with smooth stroke. Concentrate.

Photograph 4 'Take your marks' — starting positions

Photograph 5   The take off

Starts and Turns

Starts and turns are often neglected in training and consequently are performed badly in races. Every dive and turn should be considered important.

STARTS

There are many and varied ways of performing racing dives but these fall into two main categories — the stand up type and the grab start.

Of the stand up starts the most common and successful is the 'wind up' start.

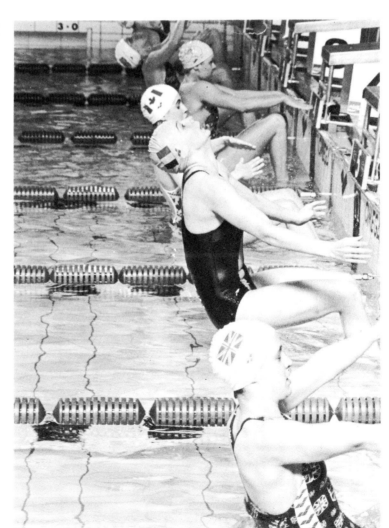

Photograph 6   Take off. Back crawl

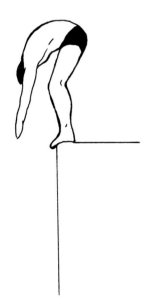

Figure 63   Stance

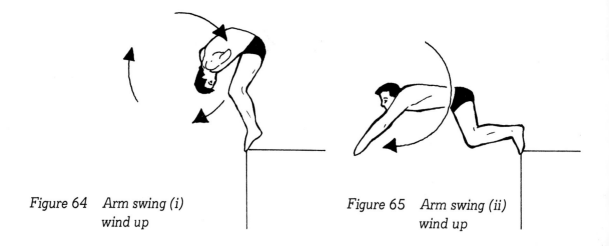

Figure 64   Arm swing (i)
wind up

Figure 65   Arm swing (ii)
wind up

WIND UP

STANCE

The toes should be curled over the edge of the starting block about hip width apart. Knees are comfortably bent with the body slightly bent forward and balanced. The arms are relaxed and pointing towards the water to the entry (figure 63 and photograph 4).

TAKE OFF

The head is dropped downwards as the arms swing forward (this causes the initial overbalancing to occur). The arms continue to swing forwards, upwards and then backwards (figure 64).

As the body drops downwards the arms, having swung in a circle, come forward in front of the body and the legs extend to take off. (This movement is a powerful explosive action) (figure 65).

FLIGHT

The body flies slightly upwards but mainly outwards. As the arms swing forward, the arm movement stops with the arms aiming at a point of entry (figure 66). The eyes, which up to now were looking well down the pool, change to look down towards the water which causes the head to drop forward between the arms (figure 67).

ENTRY

The body is now perfectly straight and aimed at the entry. (The object is to get the feet to pass through the same hole which the hands make in the water) (figure 68.)

Figure 66   Flight (i)

Figure 67   Flight (ii)

Figure 68   Entry

GLIDE

After the body enters the water, there is a short pause when the body remains stretched and streamlined, at the end of which the legs start to kick and the head is raised and the body returns to the surface.

In front crawl a single arm stroke is now taken, the recovery of which takes place without pause as the swimmer reaches the surface.

In breast stroke, the dive is somewhat deeper in the water because usually after the initial glide the swimmer completes a large sweeping movement of the arms bringing them to the sides of the body. This movement is so powerful that a second (but shorter) glide takes place underwater. After this the arms are recovered to stretch in front, as the legs propel the body to the surface.

In the butterfly stroke after the initial glide slows down, the powerful dolphin leg kick takes over and the arms complete a pull under the water. It is essential that the swimmer times the moment of surfacing to the moment when the propulsive movement of the arms finish so that they can be recovered above the water.

47

 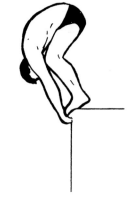 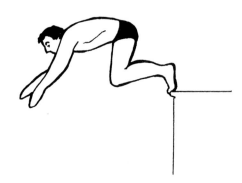

Figure 69   Stance   *Figure 70   Overbalance*   *Figure 71   Take off*

GRAB START

STANCE
The toes grip over the edge of the starting block, the knees are bent and the hands grip the block. (Some swimmers prefer to grip the block inside the feet, others outside) (figure 69.)

TAKE OFF
In the first place, the hands pull the head and shoulders downwards which causes the body to over balance (figure 70). Almost in the same action but momentarily later the hands press backwards forcing the body forwards (see photograph 5). The legs extend for take off as the body reaches the horizontal. (This movement is powerful and explosive) (figure 71.)

FLIGHT
The flight is not as spectacular as that of the stand up starts because it starts from a lower position, but it normally takes place fractionally sooner and, therefore, the swimmer hits the water sooner (figure 72).

ENTRY AND GLIDE
The aim of the entry and glide is the same in both sets of dives and that is to be as stretched and streamlined as possible (figure 73).

In modern racing dives, it is the practice to dive somewhat higher in the flight and develop piking of the body. This is done so that the legs are raised higher on entry, enabling the swimmer to have a more streamlined entry. After the entry is made, because of the steeper angle of the body, it has to flatten out quicker to reach the surface.

48

Figure 72   Flight

Figure 73   Entry

BACK STROKE START

Although it is allowed to start front crawl, butterfly and breaststroke races
in the water it is rarely attempted but back stroke races must start with the
body in the water.

STANCE

There is not a stance as such, both hands grasp the special grips which are
attached to the starting blocks. (If the blocks are not available the end of
the pool or rail may be used) and both feet are placed on the wall of the
pool, making sure that no part of the feet come above the water.

The feet need to be placed on the wall just below the surface. They may
be alongside each other at approximately hip width apart or with one foot
slightly higher than the other (figure 74).

TAKE OFF

At the moment of take off the swimmer should be well tucked and be in as
high a position as possible (figure 75).

The arms are pushed vigorously away from the blocks and the head is
pressed backwards towards the other end of the pool (figure 76 and photograph 6). The arms are now swung sideways and backwards to a stretched
position (figure 77). At the same time, the legs are thrust vigorously away
from the pool side and the body is propelled backward out of the water and
in an arched position (photograph 7).

49

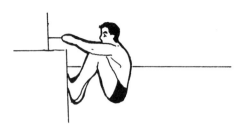

Figure 74   Stance

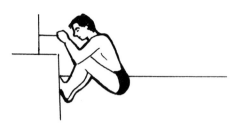

Figure 75   'Take your marks'

Figure 76   Go!

Figure 77   Flight

Photograph 7   Stretched flight over the water

FLIGHT

If the push off from the wall has been effective nearly the whole of the body is arched and in flight above the water. (It is very difficult, however, to get the lower legs out of the water) (figure 78.)

Figure 78   Entry

ENTRY AND GLIDE

The aim is exactly that of the other dives but it is virtually impossible to attain, that is to get the rest of the body to enter the same hole in the water which was made by the hands.

As the arms are entered the head is raised slightly to prevent the body from sinking too deeply. The body is stretched as it glides under water and remains so until the speeds slow to swimming speed. Then the legs are kicked vigorously followed shortly afterwards by the movement of one arm which propels the body forward. It is important that the body should reach the surface when this propelling arm has reached the hips otherwise the recovery will be restricted and so will the flow into the stroke.

TURNS

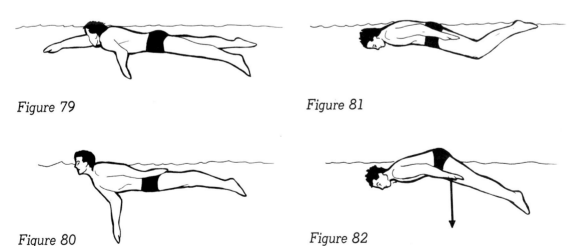

Figure 79

Figure 81

Figure 80

Figure 82

Figures 79 to 87   Front crawl tumble turn sequence

TURNS

Many vital seconds will be lost because of untidy turns. They should, there-fore, be considered as important as the swimming strokes.

FRONT CRAWL TUMBLE TURN

The tumble turn is the most effective turn used in frontcrawl. It is usually half a somersault with a quarter twist of the body added on. The amount of twist depends on the skill, speed and flexibility of the swimmer. The more twist that can be performed means that less turn is required to regain a front crawl swimming position after the push off from the wall.

APPROACH TO THE WALL

The approach to the wall is made without slowing down. The faster the speed the greater the distance away from the wall can the somersault be started.

The somersault is initiated by dropping the head on the chest at the same time both arms are pulled alongside the body. (This is usually faster if, just before the turn, one arm remains alongside the body and the other com-pletes a powerful pull push action to finish up alongside the body with palms facing the floor of the pool (figures 79, 80 and 81).

TUCK AND TWIST

It is essential at this stage for the hips to be driven upwards out of the water. The hands are pressed downwards and the legs perform a sharp downwards dolphin movement. Both of these actions have the desired effect of raising the hips (figure 82).

It is now relatively easy for the legs to tuck and swing above the water and the feet are placed on the wall sideways. Whilst this is happening, the body is
Figure 83 twisting sideways as well (figures 83, 84, 85 and 86).

Figure 84

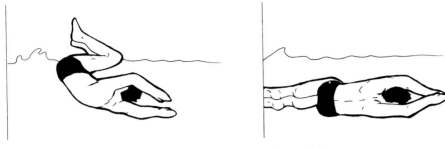

Figure 85   *Figure 86*

PUSH OFF

The arms meet and begin to stretch forward as the legs are powerfully extended off the pool wall. As the push off develops the body regains a streamlined frontal position prior to restarting the stroke (figure 87).

Figure 87

BREAST STROKE AND BUTTERFLY TURNS

These turns are almost identical in execution. The only difference is that the push off to restart swimming is deeper in the breast stroke turn.

APPROACH

The touch on the wall is made with both hands simultaneously but they do not have to be at the same level when swimming breast stroke. It is best if the touch can be timed with both arms at full extension and at fast speed (figure 88). This also applies to a good finish to a race.

Figure 88   Touch   *Figure 89   Twist off wall*   **53**

TUCK AND TWIST

After the touch is made the legs are allowed to drop and one hand is detached from the wall. The hand which is first detached sculls the body round as the other maintains contact with the wall. The legs continue to drop and are turned onto the wall. Whilst this is happening, the head is turned to face the course (figure 89).

PUSH OFF AND GLIDE

The arm which has remained on the wall is usually swung over the water, where it enters and stretches forward to join the other arm. (An alternative is to bring the arm underwater to join the stretched arm), (figure 90). While either of these two actions is taking place the legs are powerfully extended, pushing the body forward through the water to a glide, to which the first stroke is smoothly added (figures 91 and 92). The underwater movement of breast stroke at the turn is similar to the one used at the start — see page 47.

Figure 90   Turning on to front   Figure 91   Strong push off

Figure 92   Glide

BACK STROKE TURN

APPROACH

The movement into a backstroke turn usually starts with a back somersault. This movement only continues until the legs have been raised out of the water.

The leading hand is stretched on to the wall about 12 in. (30 cm) down the wall (figure 93) with the fingers pointing to the floor of the pool. The head at the same time drops back and the knees are tucked (figure 94).

Figure 93   Touch

Figure 94   Start of tuck

TUCK AND TWIST

As the legs come out of the water (figure 95), they are then carried in a twisting action so that the feet come onto the wall with the toes pointing upwards (figure 96). The hands at the same time are helping the twisting action: one with a sculling action, the other with a pushing action off the wall.

Figure 95   Somersault

Figure 96   Start of push off

PUSH OFF AND GLIDE

At this point the swimmer is almost on his back. The arms now meet beyond the head and are stretched forward and a vigorous push from the wall is executed and the back glide position is gained, onto which the kick is added and then the arm action (figure 97).

Figure 97   Glide

═══ Fundamentals of ═══ swimming training

Up to now emphasis has been placed on the techniques of swimming and, although these are important, there are other aspects which are also important if success in competition is to be achieved.

ENDURANCE

All swimming races, except for sprints of 25 metres and 50 metres, are 'endurance' events. It is important, therefore, that swimmers are fit enough to maintain good technique over longer distances than 50 metres.

In the early stages of training, a swimmer should be gradually extended to swim long distances. The initial aim should be to swim 400 metres front-crawl with reasonable technique. Other strokes should be tackled but the distance need not be so far with the possible exception of back crawl. (Care should be taken when swimming long distances on breast stroke, however, since it is such a difficult stroke to swim properly that bad habits can easily develop).

SPEED

In the early stages of training, it is debatable whether young swimmers should race over short distances. The problem is one of rushing the strokes and sacrificing good technique. Big children often make this mistake as races are often won because of size and strength.

Build-up swims are very helpful in learning how to swim faster. For example, the length of the pool can be considered as four quarters. The first quarter is swum slowly and carefully, more power is added during the second quarter, still greater power and speed of action is increased in the next quarter and the final quarter is swum at great speed but with the emphasis still on quality of stroke. The essential point is to transfer smoothly from one quarter distance to the next. As experience is increased, the pool can be divided into thirds then halves until the total distance can be swum fast with good technique.

As a young swimmer develops endurance, speed and confidence, the stage will be reached when organised training on a regular basis will be required.

The frequency, duration and intensity of these sessions should be carefully considered. Initially, 2 x 30 minute sessions per week may be sufficient for a young swimmer but at a later stage, when the swimmer has developed and matured, it may be necessary for training to extend to as much as 11 x 2 hour sessions per week.

ORGANISATION OF TRAINING

Although not all of the following items of equipment are essential, they certainly help to build confidence in the training programme.

(i) *Training clock* These should be large enough to be seen clearly. There should be one at each end of the pool and the best place for them to be stationed is on the side walls at the start and finish.

(ii) *Kick boards* These need to be large enough to give adequate support and to raise the shoulders into a realistic swimming position.

(iii) *Pull buoys* These are placed high up between the legs and should lift the hips into a realistic swimming position.

(iv) *Back stroke turning flags* These are often forgotten in training sessions but they are important in gauging and improving the turns.

(v) *Starting blocks* These are other items not often used but they are really essential for learning and improving the starts, especially the 'grab start' and back stroke starts.

(vi) *Hand paddles* These are used for strengthening the pulling muscles and they do help in improving the entry position of the hands.

(vii) *Pull tubes* These are similar to moped inner tubes and are very useful in improving strength in the pulling muscles.

(viii) *Lane dividers* These are essential when large numbers are training. They permit circuit swimming (see below) to be practised in relative safety. (There are some very sophisticated lane dividers which maintain a smooth pool at all times and hence encourage good technique.)

(ix) *Logbooks* These are important items of a swimmer's equipment in which a diary of training is kept.

CIRCUIT SWIMMING

Circuit swimming permits longer distances to be attempted in training in reasonable safety. Swimming is performed in large circles in each lane and usually in contrary directions (figure 98).

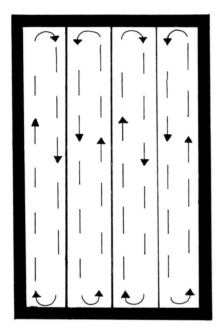

Figure 98   Circuit swimming   Figure 99   Wave swimming

WAVE SWIMMING

When speed swimming is required, swims of one length are practised. Provided the lane is wide enough, two swimmers side by side can proceed up the pool in each lane. (Care should be taken by the Coach when organising the pool in this way to allow sufficient time for the last wave to finish before the first wave turns in the opposite direction (figure 99.)

TRAINING CLOCK

When using a training clock, a swimmer should be able to see the second hand. Therefore, a clock showing a large sweeping second hand is essential. It may be helpful to include a minute hand but this is not so essential.

Inexperienced swimmers should be encouraged and constantly reminded to observe and use the clock (figure 100). Training sessions can take place without one, but these sessions are often disorganised and meaningless.

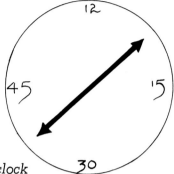

Figure 100   Training clock

A swimmer needs to be constantly aware of the time he takes to swim different distances. Only by being aware of this does a swimmer recognise improvement and gain confidence.

The clock is essential when organising rests between repetitions and there are two ways of doing this.

1   Rest for a certain length of time after a swim repeat has finished ie swim 10 x 50 metres and rest 30 seconds after each 50 metres.
2   An estimated resting time is added on to an estimated swimming time, ie swim 10 x 50 metres repeat every minute. (The Coach recognises that every swimmer will be able to swim 50 metres, have a suitable rest and begin again one minute later.)

In example 1, every swimmer has 30 seconds rest but, because the swimming times differ for each swimmer, starting times soon get mixed up which is a definite disadvantage for organised training.

In example 2, swimmers get different amounts of rest depending on their speed but the starting times are the same. Therefore, training becomes more organised.

The second method is more useful and popular when organising large groups.

When a young swimmer first starts training, it is recommended that the first swimmer in the circuit (usually called the lead swimmer) always starts when the second hand reaches 12 o'clock and the others start at five second inter-vals (ie number two always starts at five past, number three at ten past and so on).

As experience is gained, the lead swimmer will be able to start at the half past point of the clock and then quarter to and quarter past can later be added as starting points. Eventually a very experienced swimmer will be able to start at any point on the clock and be able to read off the repetition time very easily.

In certain circumstances the five seconds interval can be extended to ten seconds or reduced to three seconds. Much depends on numbers in the pool and on the experience of the swimmers.

SCHEDULES

As the ability of the swimmers improves the training, which in its early stages has been largely devoted to acquisition of good technique over longer distances, gradually progresses to organised schedules.

A schedule is the organisation of a training period to incorporate the essential requirements which swimmers need at that point in time.

A schedule, therefore, includes a main piece of work supplemented by subsidiary activities. It should have a definite purpose and have enough variety to maintain interest.

When schedules are being prepared, the main requirements are as follows: Endurance, Pace swimming, Sprinting, Technique, (applies to strokes, also starts and turns), added to which are warm ups and wind downs (when required).

While it is important for schedules to have variety, care should be taken not to include too many activities in any one schedule. The following points are strongly recommended.
(i) Decide on a main theme. It may be endurance, pace or technique.
(ii) Include some kicking and pulling.
(iii) Swim all strokes, probably in some form of Medley.
(iv) Although it is not always essential, swim front crawl in the endurance section(s) and first choice strokes in pace section(s).

ENDURANCE
Endurance is usually acquired by swimming long distances or by cutting down the distance and taking a very short rest interval.

For example a young swimmer may swim 800 metres or undertake 2 x 400 metres with 15 seconds rest or 4 x 100 metres with 10 seconds rest or 8 x

50 with 5 seconds rest. A more experienced swimmer may be asked to swim 3 x 800 with 30 seconds rest or 3 x (2 x 400 with 15 seconds) with 30 seconds rest after each set, or 3(4 x 100 with 10 seconds rest) with 30 seconds rest after each set, or 3 (8 x 50 with 5 seconds rest) with 30 seconds rest after each set.

Endurance can also be acquired by limiting the activity to either kicking or pulling.

PACE SWIMMING

Pace swimming in this instance refers to hard training as opposed to pace judgement which is an essential part of training for middle and long distance races. It is only useful when attempted by reasonably experienced swimmers. It is physically demanding especially when really fast swimming is expected and, therefore, techniques easily break down.

In this type of swimming, pace is stepped up and becomes more important. The rests between intervals are lengthened to allow the swimmer to recover more.

Pace should be increased gradually and only when the swimmer's development warrants it. It is better for young swimmers to keep the intensity relatively low rather than risk deterioration of stroke technique, which will only lead to lack of confidence.

A gradual increase of pace would develop over a period. If at first the work attempted was 20 x 100 metres rest 60 seconds, developing to 15 x 100 metres rest 1½ minutes. Then 10 x 100 metres rest 2 minutes, then 5 x 100 metres rest 3 minutes. (This type of development is only practised with experienced swimmers who will be able to improve the speed as they progress. Young swimmers would probably not progress beyond about 10 x 100 metres rest 60 seconds).

It is important to note that when attempting this type of training although not carried out at maximum speed the effort applied throughout the sets is intense.

SPRINTING

Very few opportunities exist for swimming at maximum speed and a short amount of time should be set aside for this. Distances will be short, ie 25 to 50 metres. Sprints are often organised as relay races which are excellent motivators (always check technique).

TECHNIQUE

In the early stages of training, technique work is largely controlled by a coach and takes up most of the time available. As development takes place, less and less special work is required and drills become more important see pages 42 to 44.

Technique work should never be neglected even by the most experienced swimmers and care must be ensured that it remains an important feature of training programmes.

WARM UP

The warm up section of the schedule is the first activity practised. It should be simple and easily explained. As a general rule approximately 10% of the available time is devoted to it. In the first place, it is a loosening activity then stroke awareness is practised and finally it sets the mood for the work to follow.

WIND DOWN

Wind down swims are only useful if the work has been really hard. It should be of low intensity and relaxing and should help to bring the body systems back to normality before leaving the pool.

Young swimmers who achieve enjoyment and satisfaction from swimming should consider joining one of the many swimming clubs which are affiliated to the Amateur Swimming Association through a District Association, by doing this they will be able to progress under the guidance of well qualified and experienced teachers and coaches.

In conclusion, ALL aspects mentioned in this book should receive careful attention, whether it is mental preparation, technique or fitness work. Without total preparation the ultimate goal of success will be difficult to achieve.

Useful names and addresses

Amateur Swimming Association, Harold Fern House, Derby Square, Loughborough, Leicestershire LE11 0AL

Southern – Mr E.E. Warner, 11 Warrington Road, Croydon, CR0 4BH

Midland – Mr M. Rutter, 50 Gauden Road, Pedmore, Stourbridge, West Midlands, DY9 9HN

Northern – Mr T.H. Cooper, 23 Nazeby Avenue, Great Crosby, Liverpool, L23 0SN

North-Eastern – Mr F.W. Latimer, 62 Teviotdale Gardens, Newcastle upon Tyne, NE7 7PX

Western – Mr E. Dean, 12 Kinsdale Road, Higher Street, Budeaux, Plymouth, Devon

Institute of Swimming Teachers and Coaches, Harold Fern House, Derby Square, Loughborough, Leicestershire LE11 0AL

Index